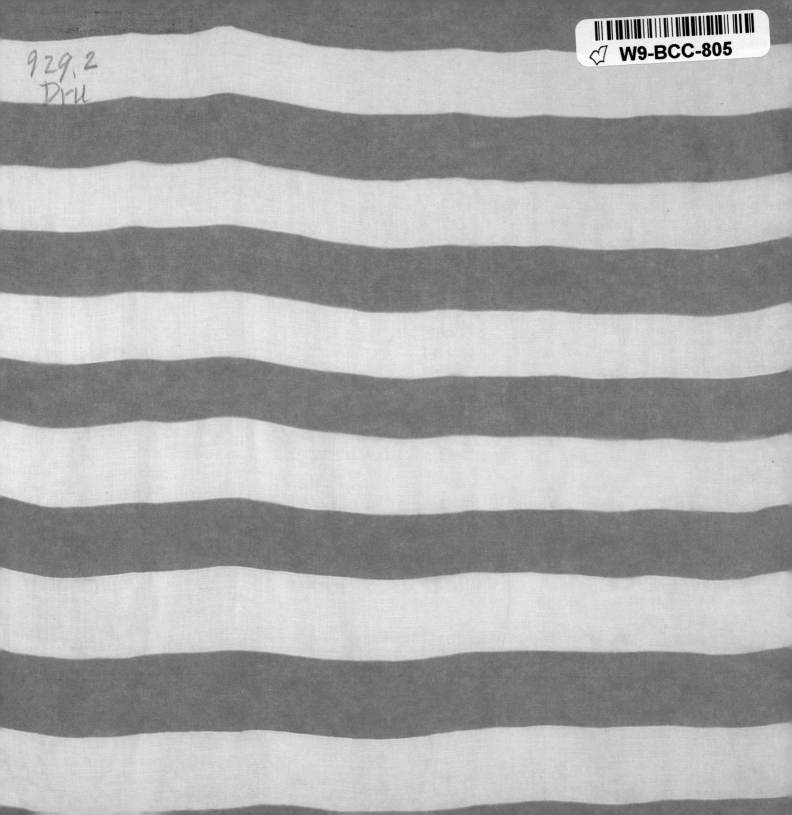

AMERICAN FLAGS

F. WILLARD

DESIGNS FOR A YOUNG NATION

N FLAGS

YOUNG NATION

F. WILLARD

By NANCY DRUCKMAN with commentaries by JEFFREY KENNETH KOHN

RAMS, INC.

PUBLISHERS

THE AMERICAN FLAG

IS A POWERFUL, ICONIC SYMBOL COM-MON TO US ALL. IT IS THE MOST ENDURING EVOCATION OF AMERICA. BUT THE CON-STANCY AND IMMUTABILITY CONVEYED BY THE PRESENT AMERICAN FLAG IS AT ODDS WITH THE HISTORY OF ITS DEVELOPMENT.

THE STORY OF HOW THE AMERICAN STAN-DARD BECAME THE AMERICAN STANDARD IS ANYTHING BUT STANDARD.

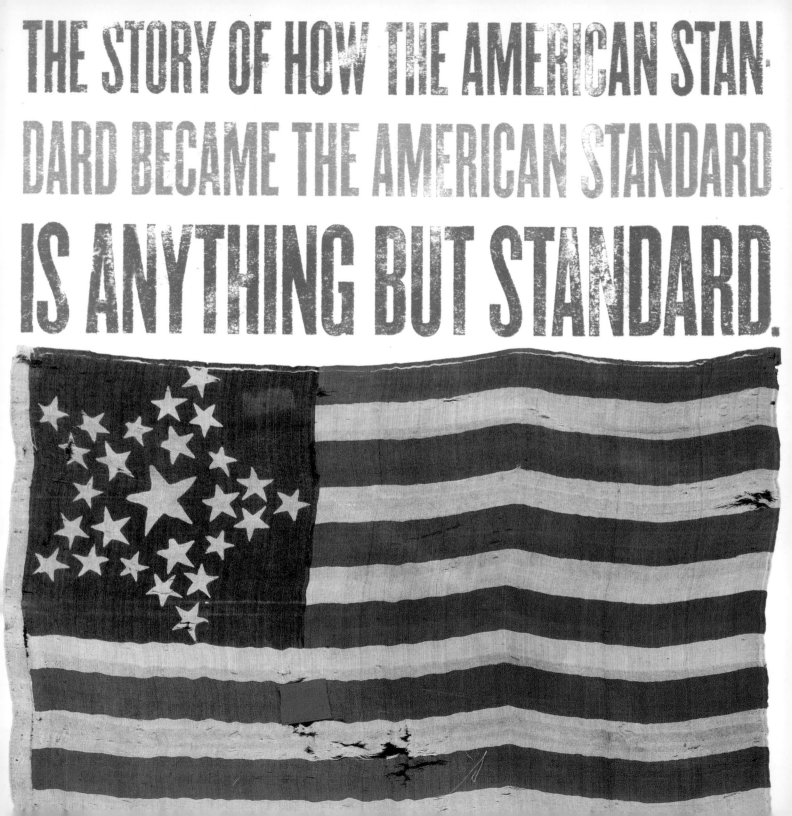

WHEN THE FOUNDING FATHERS signed the Declaration of Independence proclaiming our intentions for independence from Great Britain, their energies were devoted to the immediate priority of winning the war. The flag at that time was the Grand Union flag (see p. 12), based on the British Union Jack, with the crosses of St. George and St. Andrew in the canton—the smaller rectangular section in the upper corner next to the staff—and a field of thirteen red and white stripes to represent the thirteen colonies. It was only after a full year had elapsed that the Continental Congress recognized the need for an American flag and passed the First Flag Act on June 14, 1777. The act described the new flag in poetic, though sketchy, terms: "Resolved that a flag for the thirteen United States be thirteen stripes alternated red and white with a union of thirteen white stars in a blue field to represent a new constellation." Further details—those of size, proportion, length, shape, and arrangement of stars within the canton were left unspecified.

The task of designing this first flag was given to Frances Hopkinson, a signer of the Declaration of Independence from New Jersey. He and a committee of patriots under the direction of George Washington created the first American flag. Unfortunately, no flag, document, or painting has survived that shows exactly what that flag looked like.

In 1795, after the admission of Vermont and Kentucky into the Union, the Congress allowed both an increase of stars and stripes. Uniformity and regulation were only introduced when President Howard Taft signed an executive order in 1912. Even though the rules for formal standardization did not become law until 1912, Congress realized early on that the continuation of the practice of adding both a star and a stripe when a new state joined the Union would result in a flag whose field looked like the hair of Rapunzel. The famous Star Spangled Banner flag that flew above Fort McHenry during the War of 1812 carried fifteen stars and fifteen stripes. Six years later, in 1818, Congress decreed that a star would be added to the canton to mark a state's joining the Union, but that the number of stripes would remain at thirteen, to honor the original thirteen states.

But until 1912, the design of the American flag was in the hands of the American people—women, pioneers, patriots—for the people, by the people. What ensued was a rich and varied visual history, where the designs of the flag reflected the circumstances and events of each of the people who created them. Thus, the flag became a spontaneous and profound form of American folk art, an irrepressible expression of the creativity, ingenuity, and diversity of the country's life. The small blue canton became a "canvas" upon which expressive examples of American folk art were delineated. Bound up into each historic flag was a profound and immediate record of a moment in American history.

Flags from the early decades of the nineteenth century reflect the seafaring aspect of life in America, and the importance of the maritime industries and the navy to the wealth and security of the nation. Captain Samuel Chester Reid, a naval hero of the War of 1812, was entrusted with the design of the new flag. In the interest of visual clarity over vast expanses of open water, Captain Reid designed the "Great Star" or "Great Luminary" pattern, where the states' stars were clustered together to be read as a single blazing star. For a time, there was a move afoot to have this Great Luminary, or Great Star design, adopted as the official American flag, but President James Monroe vetoed it, mindful of unnecessary expenditures from the national budget. The cost of the change was deemed wasteful.

Examples of American flags dating from the 1820s reflect the fashion for neoclassical design. It is thought that Pierre L'Enfant, the architect of Washington, D.C., created a design of an elegant oval of thirteen stars on a blue silk ground (p. 16). Flags of the 1850s and 1860s used concentric rings or ovals of stars in the canton, called double wreaths or double medallions. The stars were either uniformly positioned or scattered, and they could be either fat or skinny. The arrangement could suggest a starburst or a flower; it could be static or evoke the poetry of motion.

Flags of the Civil War era were of great size—to decorate large public gathering places and inspire the crowds that rallied there. The guidon flag also came into use during the Civil War: The V-shaped swallowtail was aeronautically designed to fly straight, allowing the cavalry troops riding behind the standard to stay in formation (pp. 47–49).

A flag from the border state of Kansas (p. 39) embedded the Southern Cross, an emblem of the Confederacy, into a canton of the regulation thirty-four stars, its alternating red and white stripes reduced to nine to honor the nine states seceding from the Union. This became a "sanctuary flag" indicating safe harbor for members of the Confederacy wherever this flag was flown.

In the post–Civil War era, flags were integrated into everyday life. They were used for less exalted purposes than those for which they were employed during the Civil War, including the commonplace concerns of the marketplace and politics. General Ulysses S. Grant and his running mate, Schuyler Colfax, affixed labels printed with their names on the thirty-four-star Kansas flag for their 1868 bid for the Presidency. Later in the nineteenth century, the flag was printed with advertising for everything from fishing tackle, "Magnolia-brand" Virginia ham, hats, ties, and trunks.

In contrast to the crass and commercial, the flag could express immediate and intimate poignancy. The World War I "Peace Flag" was a small, printed cotton Bible flag, made in a small size so that it could be carried into battle in Europe by an American soldier. The rain-soaked example shown in this book (p. 78) was inscribed along the bottom by that soldier: *First Train with American Prisoners of War Passed Through Lausanne on Friday, Nov. 29th, 1918.*

At every turn, the American flag reflects significant moments in our history and culture, a shared moment in the national consciousness. Like other examples of American folk art, the early flag displays creativity, imagination, ingenuity, and inspiration—the freedom that underlies American life. Today, as in the past, the American flag is a symbol of poignancy and power. It reminds us of our shared history, common purpose, and hopes for the future.

NANCY DRUCKMAN

★

American flags normally have three parts: the main expanse of the flag, or *field*, generally emblazoned with alternating red and white horizontal stripes; the *canton,* a smaller rectangular area in the upper left corner of the banner next to the staff; and the *sleeve,* or *heading,* a band of cloth that reinforces the edge where the flag is attached to its support. If ropes or cords are used to support the flag, the sleeve will often contain *grommets,* reinforced eyelets through which the cords can be passed. The end where the sleeve is attached is called the *hoist*; the far end is called the *fly.* ☆ As we shall see, historic flags may be either commercially manufactured or homemade; homemade examples are sometimes highly idiosyncratic, but even the commercially made ones may be irregularly laid out or otherwise have a distinctly "folk-art" look to them.

It should be noted that because of their large size some flags pictured in this book were folded horizontally and/or vertically before being photographed.

THE AMERICAN GRAND UNION OR CONTINENTAL FLAG

If George Washington flew a flag while in camp or on his historic crossing of the Delaware, it would have been one of this design. The flag shown here is the only known example surviving from the late eighteenth century or early nineteenth century of the standard that represented the thirteen English colonies of North America before they separated from the mother country. Known as the American Grand Union or Continental flag, it featured a field of thirteen red and white stripes to represent each of the colonies, and a canton—the smaller rectangular section in the upper corner next to the staff—configured in the form of the British Union Jack. The canton stripes are a hand-sewn combination of homespun cotton and silk.

GEORGE WASHINGTON'S INAUGURAL BANNER

This historic shield banner is believed to have been suspended from the balcony above George Washington at Federal Hall in New York City during his 1789 inauguration as the first President of the United States. The thirteen cotton muslin stars were sewn by hand on the blue wool bunting crest, while the face of the shield was emblazoned with thirteen red and white vertical stripes. The entire shield was then sewn onto a panel pieced together from four sections of white wool bunting.

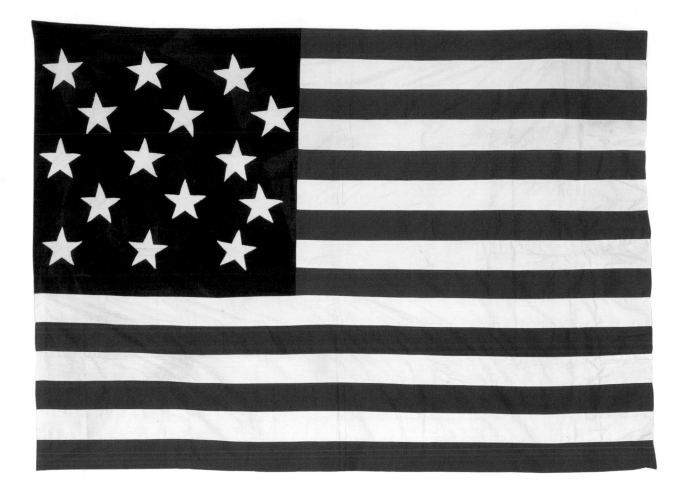

THE STAR-SPANGLED BANNER

This homemade banner made for the 1876 Centennial of American independence is a replica of the fifteen-star, fifteen-stripe flag that inspired Francis Scott Key to write the American National Anthem during the War of 1812. Returning from a trip to Baltimore in August 1814 to negotiate the release of a friend who had been taken prisoner by the British, Key watched the bombardment of Fort McHenry by the Royal Navy from a boat in Baltimore Harbor. It was this experience that resulted in his writing the poem that later became the patriotic hymn.

To celebrate the 1876 Centennial of American independence, many Americans made replicas of historic flags like this one for exhibition. This particular example is of cotton, with hand-sewn stars in horizontal rows and machine-sewn stripes. The fact that the canton rests on a white stripe is unusual; normally in flags of this period the canton rests on a red stripe.

A "STARBURST" FLAG TO COMMEMORATE ILLINOIS STATEHOOD

This unique flag, whose twenty-one stars seem to be exploding from the canton in a burst of progressively larger lights, was made to commemorate the admission of Illinois to the Union on December 3, 1818. The large central star represents Illinois itself, the twenty-first state. The uppermost stripe is white, a feature rare in American flags but commonly found in banners in European heraldry, which suggests that the maker may have been a recent immigrant. This may also explain why the canton, unusually, rests on a red stripe. The scarcity of wool-silk blended cloth in the early nineteenth century may account for the fact that this flag has only eleven stripes.

AN EARLY NINETEENTH-CENTURY FLAG

This thirteen-star flag probably dates to the first quarter of the nineteenth century. The stars are arranged in a diamond formation with a star at its center and flanked by four more stars set at the corners of the canton. The nine stripes of the field are not unusual for flags of this period; throughout the nineteenth century it was common to find flags with nine, ten, eleven, twelve, or fourteen stripes rather than the thirteen that had been legislated by the First Flag Act of June 14, 1777 and the Third Flag Act of April 4, 1818. Flag-makers may not have been aware of the legislation, or perhaps the freedom of their designs was simply an expression of their individual tastes. Here, the canton and stripes are hand-sewn wool bunting; the stars are hand-sewn cotton muslin.

MAJOR L'ENFANT'S FLAG

In 1783, Major Pierre L'Enfant, the designer of the city of Washington, was asked to provide a drawing to decorate the parchment membership document, or diploma, of the newly founded patriotic Society of the Cincinnati. The flag shown here, which dates to the first quarter of the nineteenth century, repeats the design of the flag shown in L'Enfant's drawing for that commission. In this elegant rendition, thirteen gilt-painted stars are set in an oval on a hand-sewn silk canton. The stripes are also hand-sewn silk.

A UNIQUE FLAG IN
THE STYLE OF THE 1820s

When General Marquis de La Fayette made a return visit to America in 1824, the diary entries of some observers describe "houses in New York . . . and Washington being festooned with flags." The thirteen-star flag shown here may well date from that period, although it may have been made sometime later, possibly as late as 1850. The pattern of the stars in the canton—a row of five stars above two rows of four stars each—is unique. The irregularity of the alignment of each row and the orientation of the individual stars vary considerably, giving this banner the appearance of a work of folk art. The stars are hand-sewn cotton muslin; the canton is of wool bunting.

A FLAG COMMEMORATING
ARKANSAS'S STATEHOOD

This flag was found with its original sailcloth canvas carrying bag, which suggests that it was used at sea. The canton features twenty-four stars arranged in an elongated oval around a huge central star representing Arkansas, which was admitted into the Union as our twenty-fifth state on June 15, 1836. The stars are hand-sewn cotton muslin; the canton and stripes are of wool bunting and the sleeve is made of linen with two whipstitched grommets. Only a few flags of this vintage have survived, which suggests that this one was held to be of great importance by its former owners.

A "KINGS BORO" PAINTED EAGLE FLAG, CA. 1837

The canton of this flag is emblazoned with a large painted spread-winged eagle clutching a ribbon inscribed *E. Pluribus Unum*, superimposed on a large painted sunburst. Overarching the eagle against a painted sky are twenty-six stars, arranged in three tiers of graduated sizes. On the eagle's breast is a painted shield containing thirteen alternating red and white stripes. Among the eagle's feathers below the shield is painted the name *Holmes*, most likely the painter of the flag. Below the eagle is a banner inscribed *Kings Boro*, possibly referring to the city (now the borough) of Brooklyn, New York.

One nineteenth-century design for flags—rarely found but popular with collectors today—gathered the stars on the canton in a large star configuration, called the "Great Star" or "Great Luminary" pattern. There was support in some quarters for a version of this configuration to be adopted as the official form of the national flag. Indeed Captain Samuel Chester Reid, a naval hero from the War of 1812, approached President James Monroe with the proposal to make the national flag more easily recognizable at sea from a distance by adopting just such a "Great Luminary" form. Owing to the fabrication costs of the design Captain Reid's proposal was not approved, however the "Great Star" pattern was still occasionally used throughout the nineteenth century.

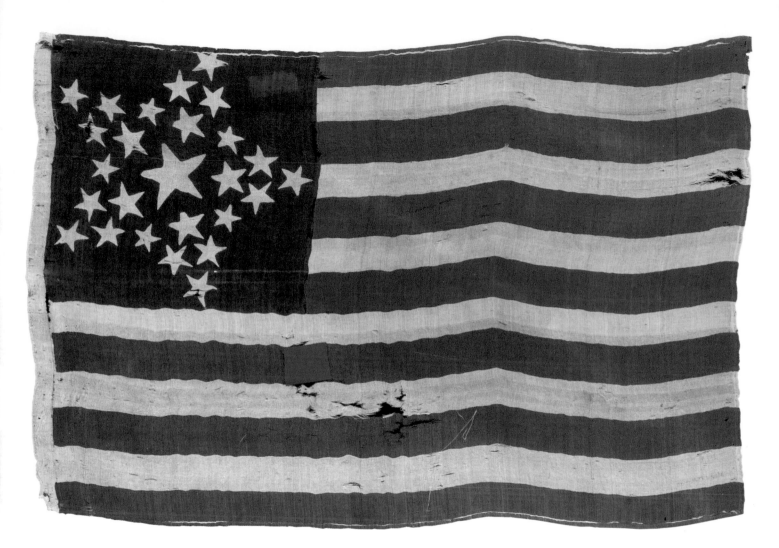

AN EARLY PRINTED "GREAT STAR" PARADE FLAG, CA. 1837

Parade flags were ephemeral—made to be used only once during a specific event and then discarded. This rare surviving example from the early nineteenth century features twenty-six stars to commemorate the admission of Michigan to the Union in 1837. The various-sized stars are configured in the "Great Star" or "Great Luminary" pattern, with the large central star representing the new state. The fact that the vertical axis of the "Great Star" is tilted gives this flag both a vivid dynamism and something of the quality of folk art.

Printed on silk, this flag is one of the earliest surviving examples of a printed parade flag. Only four or five others are known from this period.

A "GREAT STAR" FLAG TO HONOR MICHIGAN'S STATEHOOD

This twenty-six-star American national flag commemorates Michigan's admission to the Union on January 26, 1837. The hand-sewn cotton muslin stars are set in a "Great Star" or "Great Luminary" pattern with the central, equal-sized star representing the new state. The stripes are hand-sewn wool bunting.

This early parade flag commemorates Michigan's admission to the Union in 1837. Its twenty-six stars are configured in a tilted "Great Star" or "Great Luminary" pattern, with the stars radiating in diminishing size outward from a larger central star representing the new state. Printed on cotton, it is the only example of a printed parade flag of this design known.

THE GILDERSLEEVE METEOR CONSTELLATION FLAG (ABOVE)

This homemade flag, created to commemorate the admission of Michigan to the Union in 1837, presents its stars in a unique configuration against a pieced-together blue canton. Adding to its "folk art" quality, and showing more enthusiasm than foresight, the maker sewed one of the stars on so that it partially overlaps the white stripe just below the canton. The sleeve is inscribed *S. Gildersleve*, and one of the stars also bears the inscription *Gilder*. A former owner of the flag, who thought the grouping of the stars resembled a meteor shower, dubbed it the "Gildersleeve Meteor Constellation."

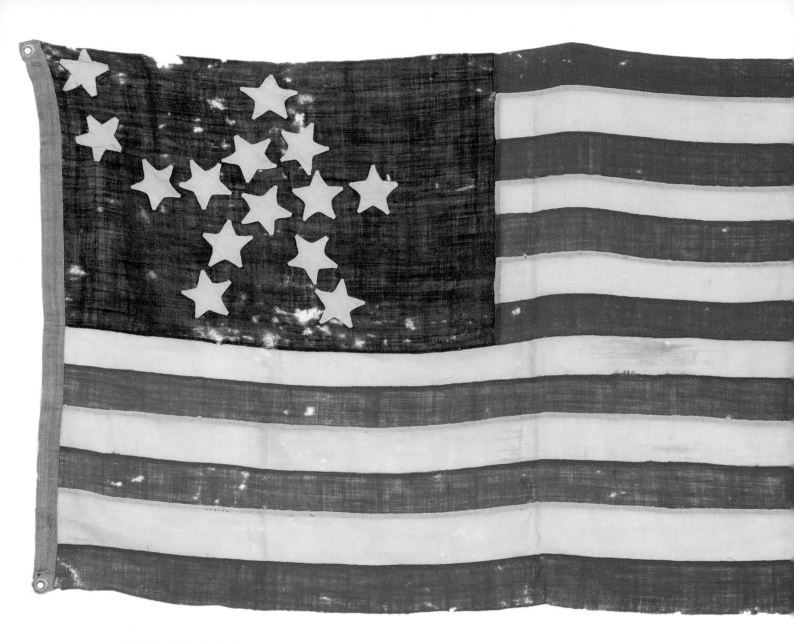

VERMONT'S UNIQUE VARIANT OF THE "GREAT STAR" FLAG, CA. 1840—60

One of the most unusual commercially made flags seen to date, this example is one of only three or four fourteen-star flags known. The hand-sewn cotton muslin stars are set in a unique "Great Star" or "Great Luminary" pattern, with one arm extending upward. It was very probably carried by soldiers from Vermont, our fourteenth state, into battle during the Civil War.

This twenty-eight-star flag was made to honor Texas's admission to the Union on December 29, 1845. The stars, set in a "Great Star" or "Great Luminary" pattern, are not only irregularly laid out, but are also tilted to the left—an arrangement that gives this hand-sewn cotton flag a pronounced "folk" appearance.

This thirty-one-star parade flag commemorates California's admission to the Union on September 9, 1850. Printed on glazed muslin, it features stars set into a double-medallion or wreath pattern, with the large central star representing the new state. The central star is also double-haloed for further emphasis. Parade flags from this period are rare.

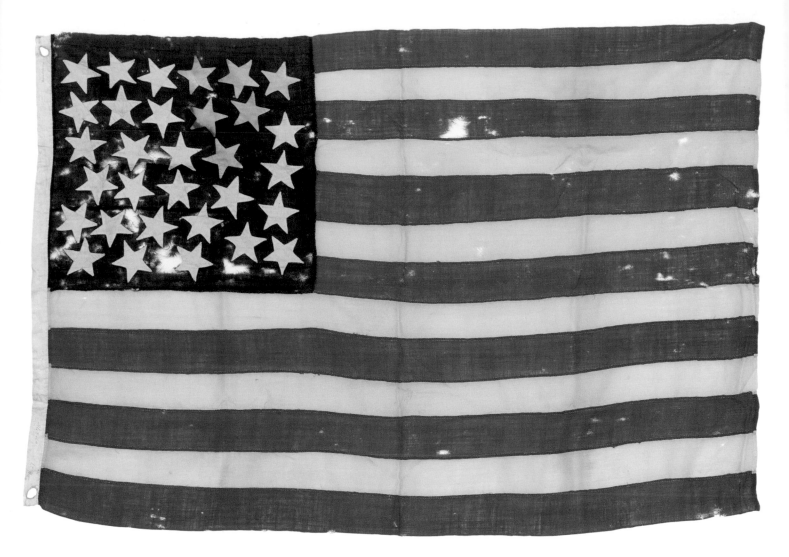

A HOMEMADE CALIFORNIA STATEHOOD FLAG

This thirty-one-star homemade flag commemorates California's admission to the Union in 1850. The stars are scattered across the canton in a pattern with no recognizable geometric form, and the stripes are of varying widths, which gives the banner a decidedly "folkey" quality. The hand-sewn stars are cotton muslin; the stripes are wool bunting.

A "GREAT STAR" CALIFORNIA PARADE FLAG

This thirty-one-star parade flag printed on cotton muslin commemorates California's admission to the Union in 1850. Its stars are configured in the "Great Star" or "Great Luminary" pattern with the largest central star representing California and stars progressively decreasing in size radiating outward. Parade flags like this one were generally printed cheaply on wool, cotton, or silk, attached to a small staff, used once, and then discarded, which accounts for their relative rarity.

AN AMERICAN "INDIAN PEACE FLAG," CA. 1850

While the standard American "Stars and Stripes" emblem held little meaning for Native Americans, the eagle was a powerful symbol for them. Thus, as a means of winning the loyalty of Native American chiefs, and as a token of peace with them, the Federal Government presented them with flags with an eagle on the canton. This hand-sewn example is one of only five such peace flags known. The thirteen overarching stars and the eagle are cotton muslin; the shield is hand-sewn silk.

A "THIRD MARYLAND" FLAG FROM THE MID-NINETEENTH CENTURY

The arrangement of the stars on this flag—a wreath surrounding a large central star—is known as the "Third Maryland" pattern because it was first used during the Revolutionary War by a regiment of Maryland soldiers. Thirteen-star flags were used officially from the time of the Revolutionary War until 1916, when President Woodrow Wilson wrote an executive order ending their use—and severing a historic link with our country's past. On this example, the stars are hand-sewn cotton muslin; the canvas sleeve or heading contains a period hemp rope with a wooden toggle, which suggests nautical use.

A KNOW-NOTHING AMERICAN POLITICAL PARTY FLAG, CA. 1858

The Know-Nothing Party flourished briefly begin-ning in 1852. A xenophobic, anti-Catholic, nativist organization, it was founded in response to the waves of Irish and German immigrants who were arriving in the country. The party's name came from the response its members gave when asked about the organization, which was "I know nothing." The unusual canton of this flag is a hand-sewn cotton medallion depicting George Washington below a flag-bearing eagle, above which are embroidered in red thread thirteen seven-pointed stars. The remainder of the flag consists of eight narrow red cotton bands sewn onto a single piece of white cotton, the lower of which is embroidered with initials and the date *1858*.

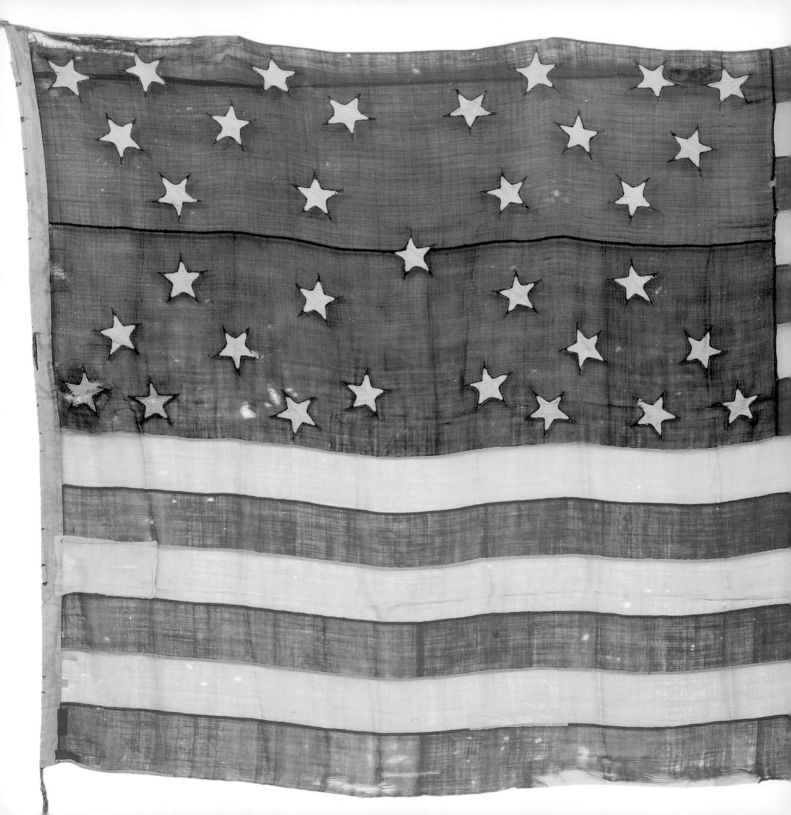

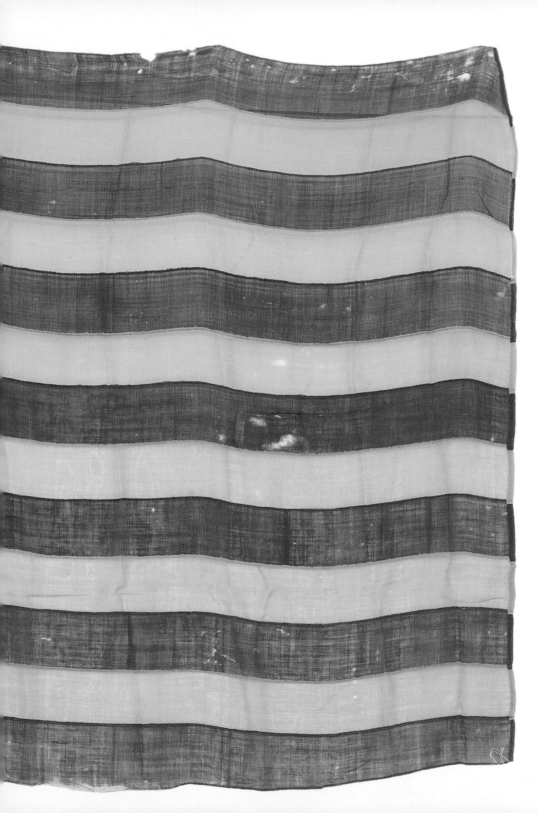

A FLAG TO COMMEMORATE THE STATEHOOD OF OREGON

This is a unique flag, made by hand to celebrate the admission of Oregon to the Union on February 14, 1859, as our thirty-third state. The canton has been pieced together from two sections of blue wool bunting with cotton muslin stars. The distinctive configuration of stars in successive curves has prompted one writer to call it the "parenthesis flag."

These flags are said to have been carried by delegates from the indicated states at the 1860 Republican convention in Chicago, at which Abraham Lincoln was nominated for the presidency. The stars are configured in a tilted "Great Star" or Great Luminary" pattern with a star in each of the spaces between the star's points. The flags are printed on polished cotton, each with a state's name painted across the eighth and ninth stripes. The red stripes in these examples have oxidized to a mellow salmon color.

A THIRTEEN-STAR HOMEMADE AMERICAN NATIONAL FLAG, CA. 1860—76 (ABOVE)

Some collectors believe that flags like this one, with only seven stripes, were sewn by soldiers or seamstresses sympathetic to the Southern cause during the Civil War, noting that initially there were seven states loyal to the Confederacy. Here the thirteen hand-sewn stars are arranged in a wreath surrounding a large central star flanked by four corner stars and sewn on a polished cotton canton. The stars are cotton muslin; the white stripes are cotton; the red are of a copper-printed flat brocade.

A FLAG USED IN LINCOLN'S CAMPAIGN

This thirty-one-star flag, which commemorates California's admission to the Union in 1850, was discovered in the loft of a barn on land that later became Cherry Hill, New Jersey. Found with it was a nineteenth-century hand-written placard (see illustration) stating, *This flag was unfurled during the first Lincoln* [presidential] *campaign, 1860.* It was the practice then, as it is today, to display an older flag when a more current example was not available. The hand-sewn cotton muslin stars are set in a double-oval medallion on a wool bunting canton.

A HOMEMADE FLAG
HONORING KANSAS STATEHOOD

This thirty-four-star flag commemorates Kansas's admission to the Union on January 29, 1861, as the thirty-fourth state. Its maker tried to arrange the stars in a double-oval medallion, but plainly had difficulty fitting all the stars onto the unusually small canton. The jumbled star configuration and the elongated stripes together give the flag a decided "folk art" appearance. The large central element is an eight-sided rowel star, which suggests that the seamstress was probably a recent immigrant from Europe living in Kansas when the territory became a state.

This is the canton of a thirty-four-star flag that commemorates the admission to the Union of Kansas on January 29, 1861. The hand-sewn cotton muslin stars are configured in a classic "Great Star" or "Great Luminary" pattern. The stripes, which are hand-sewn wool bunting, are folded behind the canton. Although this star configuration is one of the rarest, it was not unusual to see flags of this design carried by soldiers into battle during the Civil War.

A UNIQUE "SOUTHERN CROSS" FLAG HONORING KANSAS STATEHOOD (ABOVE)

The plump, starfishlike stars on this thirty-four-star flag that commemorates Kansas's statehood are arranged in a unique version of the "Southern Cross" pattern commonly found on flags of the Confederate States of America. Also atypically, the canton rests on a red rather than white stripe. Some flag collectors call this red stripe the "war" or "blood" stripe, believing that its position immediately beneath the canton signifies that the nation was at war when the flag was made. The nine stripes may represent the nine states of the Confederacy, thus indicating the sympathies of the banner's maker. The flag is entirely of hand-sewn cotton, with a canton of very rare cornflower blue. The red stripes have faded to a deep salmon color.

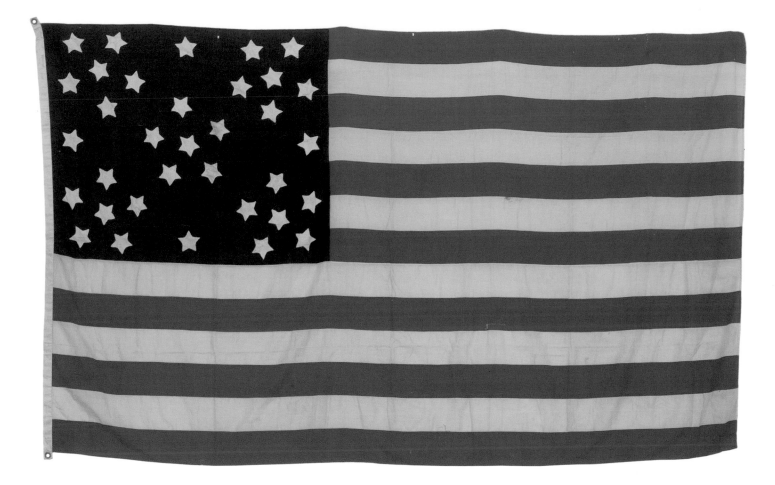

A "FLOWER" OR "BOW-TIE" PATTERN FLAG TO HONOR KANSAS'S STATEHOOD

The stars of this flag, whose thirty-four stars commemorate the admission of Kansas to
the Union in 1861, are configured in a very rare "flower" or "bow-tie" pattern on a two-
piece wool-silk blend canton. The canton, wool-silk blend stripes, and cotton sleeve are
hand-sewn. In the sleeve are two brass grommets.

AN UNUSUALLY LARGE FLAG HONORING KANSAS STATEHOOD

Because of the large size of this flag—approximately twelve feet high and twenty-four feet long—the canton had to be made from five pieces of wool bunting. Wool bunting was not manufactured in larger widths in the United States in 1861, the year Kansas was admitted to the Union. In fact, until 1867, flag-makers imported their blue wool bunting from England. Here the thirty-four cotton muslin stars were hand-sewn in an outer oval wreath surrounding an inner circular wreath that encloses a large central star to represent the new state.

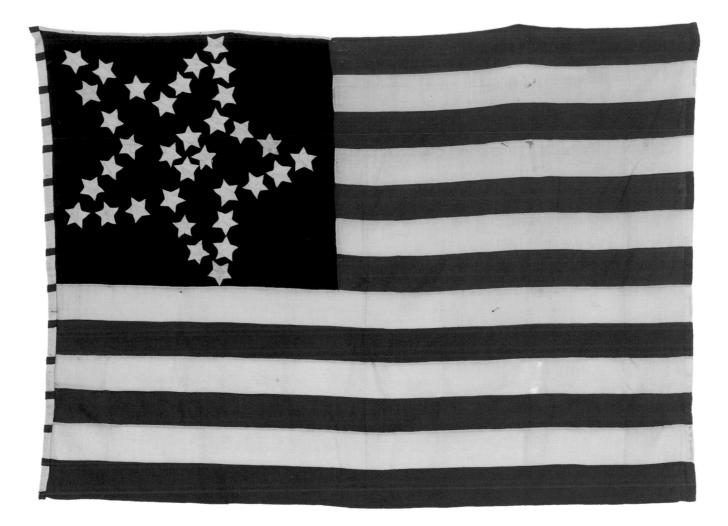

A "GREAT STAR" FLAG HONORING KANSAS STATEHOOD

This thirty-four-star flag commemorates Kansas's admission to the Union in 1861. The hand-sewn cotton muslin stars are set in a slightly tilted "Great Star" or "Great Luminary" pattern, enclosing four stars within it. The canton and red stripes are of wool-silk blend and the white stripes are wool; all are hand-sewn. There is a wool twill tape sewn along the top of the canton and first stripe, and additional wool twill tape stripes along the sleeve, a feature that gives this flag a distinctly "folk art" quality.

Flags in the nineteenth century might be emblazoned with political mottoes, as is the case with this thirty-four-star Kansas flag dating to the early 1860s. Here, the cotton sleeve is painted with the words *Our Policy The Will Of The People*. Unfortunately, the candidate, party, or movement for which the banner was made remains a mystery. The hand-sewn cotton muslin stars are set in straight rows on a wool bunting canton; the stripes are hand-sewn wool bunting. Not surprisingly, political banners, which were usually made for short-term use, have only rarely survived.

A HOMEMADE OHIO CIVIL WAR BATTLE FLAG

This unique seventeen-star flag was made to be carried by soldiers in a regiment from Ohio—the seventeenth state—into battle during the Civil War. The unusual eight-pointed stars suggests that the banner was designed by someone who had recently immigrated from Europe; their form closely resembles a rowel, the mul- tipointed wheel of a knight's spur, a device that appears commonly in medieval heraldry. The canton is partic- ularly striking for its scattered arrangement of stars, which look as if they had been thrown at random onto the blue field and sewn wherever they landed. The flag is entirely of hand-sewn cotton.

A "BOXED MEDALLION" INDIANA COMMEMORATIVE FLAG

Flags like this nineteen-star banner were made during the Civil War for soldiers who came from the states the flags com- memorated, in this case, Indiana. The eleven stripes may indicate the maker's sympathy to the Confederate cause, since there were nine states loyal to the Con- federacy and two border states, Missouri and Kansas. The stars are set in a "boxed medallion" pattern—a wreath or medal- lion of six stars surrounding a central star, all of which are enclosed within a square of twelve stars. The entire flag is machine-sewn cotton.

Guidons are small flags carried by troops to show the position of the guide or line on which a military formation is to be made. They also help distinguish one regiment from another. Their swallowtail form allows them to fly straight in windy conditions so that they can be easily read at a distance.

A KANSAS GUIDON, CA. 1861—63

Swallowtailed guidons like this thirty-four-star Kansas example were used during the Civil War to help guide cavalry troops during maneuvers. The gilt-painted stars are configured in a double medallion or wreath pattern surrounding the letter "L" outlined in black and red on a pale blue canton. The exact meaning of the letter "L" is unclear although it may represent the Roman numeral fifty. The canton, stripes, and fringe are all hand-sewn silk. A similar flag is in the collection of the National Military Academy at West Point.

TWO WEST VIRGINA GUIDONS, CA. 1863

These thirty-five-star guidons commemorate West Virginia's admission to the Union on June 20, 1863. Like the Kansas example (opposite), they are cut in a swallowtail form, for ease of legibility during battle. One of these, inscribed on its first white stripe, *Presented to Julia R. Hunt by Her Friend Cassius*, was probably presented to the lady named by a Union officer to celebrate the Northern victory. The stars are gilt-painted in a double-medallion pattern on a machine-sewn silk canton.

The stripes are made of machine-sewn silk.

There is considerable confusion today about the forms of Confederate flags, partly because many Southern generals designed their own flags, and partly because the Congress of the Confederate States adopted three different official flags to represent the Southern states during the course of the Civil War. The Confederate flag best known today—the familiar horizontal banner bearing a blue St. Andrew's Cross emblazoned with stars and set on a red background—is actually the jack of the Confederate Navy. A square version of this flag was adopted by General Robert E. Lee as the standard of the Army of Northern Virginia, and thus became the Confederate battle flag best known to many Union soldiers. ✫ In 1861 the Congress of the Confederate States of America adopted a flag bearing three wide horizontal stripes—a white stripe between two red ones—and a blue canton with stars on it to represent the Confederate states. Surviving examples of this flag, known as the First Confederate National flag or the

"Stars and Bars" (see pp. 52 and 53), show that the number and configuration of the stars could vary a great deal, depending on the designer's taste and how many states were considered loyal to the Confederacy at the time the flag was made. ☆ In 1863 the Confederate Congress adopted a second flag, a white banner with a canton derived from the Confederate Navy Jack, that is, the now-familiar blue St. Andrew's Cross with stars on it against a red field. However, the Confederate soldiers detested this flag, whose large expanse of white resembled, they thought, a white flag of surrender. To distinguish it from that ignominious association, many soldiers dipped this flag's fly end in blood so that there could be no mistake about its meaning. ☆ In 1864 the Confederate congress adopted a third official flag, this one incorporating the soldiers' alteration of the second flag: a red "blood" stripe running the length of the fly end. A good example of this Third Confederate National flag is shown on page 54. ☆

Small flags like this one, which measures 12¾ x 21¼ inches, were often sewn by a Confederate soldier's mother, wife, or sweetheart for him to carry in his Bible or wallet during the Civil War. This First Confederate National flag features eleven stars set in a pattern of two concave vertical columns flanking a slightly tilted column, and three stripes. The entire flag is hand-sewn cotton.

THE "STARS AND BARS," CA. 1861 (ABOVE)

This is an early example of the First Confederate National flag, known as the "Stars and Bars." The stars represent the seven states loyal to the Confederacy when this flag was sewn. The hand-sewn stars are set in a circle or wreath on a wool bunting canton. The three hand-sewn stripes are wool bunting. The linen sleeve or heading bears the ink inscription, *Savannah/May 1861.*

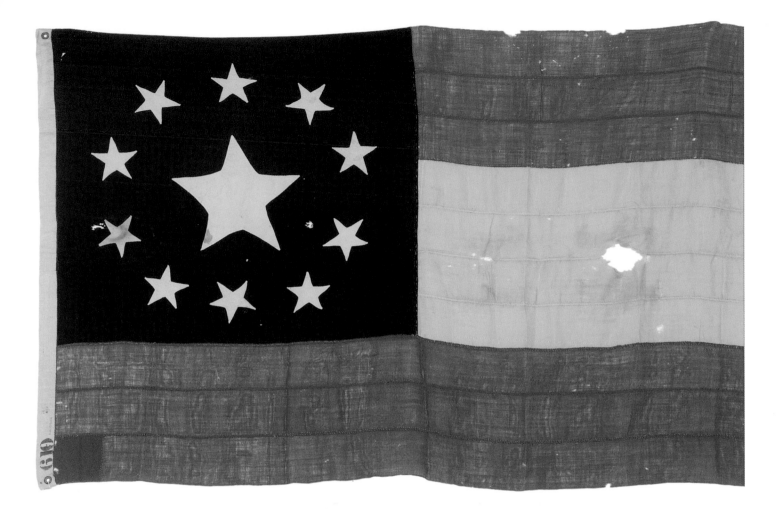

AN ELEVEN-STAR FIRST CONFEDERATE NATIONAL FLAG, CA, 1861—65

The hand-sewn stars on this flag are arranged in a wreath surrounding a very large central star on a wool-silk blend canton; the stripes are wool bunting. It is not uncommon to find "Stars and Bars" First Confederate National flags with seven, nine, eleven, or even twelve stars representing the various states loyal to the Confederacy, including "border states" such as Kansas or Missouri.

A CONFEDERATE VETERANS FLAG, LATE 1890s (BELOW)

This flag was made to be used in parades and celebrations by Confederate Civil War veterans, These survivors of the war founded a group called the United Confederate Veterans in the late 1890s and probably used this flag, which is a Third Confederate National flag, the third flag adopted by the Congress of the Confederate States of America in 1864. It features the "Southern Cross" star configuration printed on a glazed red muslin canton, which is sewn to white wool bunting with a single red stripe on the fly end of the flag.

A FIRST CONFEDERATE NATIONAL FLAG, CA. 1861—63 (ABOVE)

During the Civil War, groups of Confederate ladies made patriotic and inspirational flags for their men to carry into battle. Here, there are twelve stars on the canton, embroidered onto which is the phrase *God Armeth the Patriot.* The canton and stripes are wool bunting, the stars cotton muslin. The entire flag is hand-sewn, with the fringe now missing from the fly end.

A THIRTEEN-STAR FLAG, CA. 1865

On this flag the thirteen stars are set in symmetrically arranged straight rows. Across the mid-section of the banner a vertical cotton band has been sewn, with the following words stenciled on it in ink: *The Old Flag of the War 1861–5.* During the nineteenth century, it was not uncommon for flags to be decorated with bands bearing hand-lettered commemorative inscriptions or mottoes. On this example, the cotton muslin stars are hand-sewn; the canton and stripes are machine-sewn wool bunting.

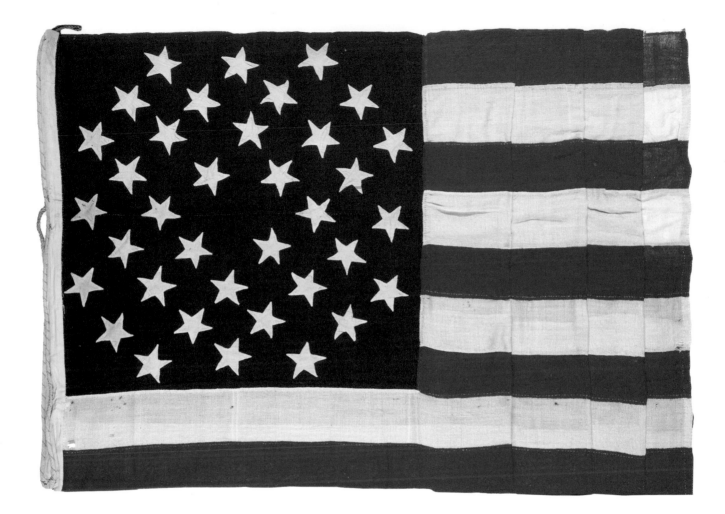

A UNIQUE FLAG TO HONOR THE STATEHOOD OF NEVADA, 1864—67

This thirty-six-star flag commemorates Nevada's admission to the Union on October 31, 1864. Although Nevada became a state while the Civil War was in progress, its membership in the Union was not officially recognized by Congress until July 4, 1865, several months after the war was over. The hand-sewn cotton muslin stars are configured in a unique truncated diamond pattern on a pieced hand-sewn wool bunting canton. The wool bunting stripes are also hand-sewn. Because of the flag's large size, the illustration here shows it partially folded.

A "GREAT STAR" FLAG TO HONOR NEVADA

This thirty-six-star flag commemorates Nevada's admission to the Union in 1864. The white painted stars are configured in a tilted "Great Star" or "Great Luminary" design with a larger central star representing the new state on a light blue silk canton. The stripes are hand-sewn silk.

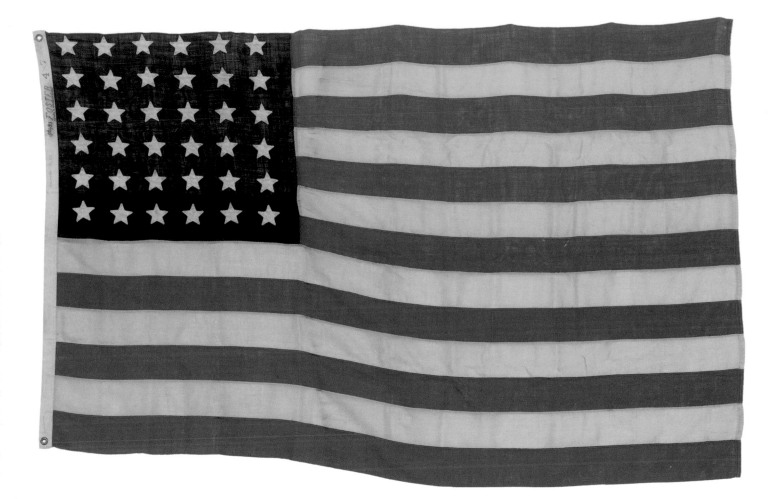

A FLAG PRESENT AT THE OPENING OF THE BROOKLYN BRIDGE, CA. 1864–83

It has always been acceptable and customary to fly or carry an older-vintage flag with a star count from an earlier period when an up-to-date flag is not available. It seems that the owner did so in this case. Although this thirty-six-star flag was almost certainly made earlier than 1883, its canvas sleeve bears the following ink inscription: *5/24/83 FOSTER/Opening of the NY & Bklyn Bridge*. The cotton muslin stars, set in straight rows on a pieced blue wool bunting canton, are machine-sewn. The wool bunting stripes and canvas sleeve are hand-sewn.

Sewn to the sleeve of this thirty-seven-star flag is a cotton band inscribed with the words *Equal Taxation*, the motto of Horatio Seymour, the unsuccessful Democratic presidential candidate in 1868. The stars are arranged in a double-medallion or wreath pattern containing an equal-sized central star, which represents Nebraska. The canton and stripes are wool bunting; the stars and sleeve are cotton muslin, with the sleeve containing nine brass grommets. The entire flag is hand-sewn.

REVENUE CUTTER FLAGS

The Revenue Cutter Service was established by an act of Congress in 1790 to patrol the American coasts and prevent smuggling. In 1915, the Service was combined with the Light House Establishment and the Life Saving Service to form the United States Coast Guard. Nineteenth-century Revenue Cutter Service flags display an eagle on the canton. They are the only official American flags that display vertical stripes.

✦

A THIRTY-SIX-STAR AMERICAN EAGLE JACK, SECOND HALF OF THE NINETEENTH CENTURY

Nautical jacks like this one were used on Revenue Cutter Service ships, and also on private vessels, as can be seen in nineteenth-century marine paintings. Here, the wool-silk blend spread-winged eagle is sewn onto a pieced canton of cream-colored wool bunting. On the eagle's breast is a shield bearing three stars over seven vertical stripes. Surrounding the eagle are four equally positioned slate blue wool-silk blend stars, each of which is separated by an additional eight red-dyed cotton muslin stars.

A UNITED STATES REVENUE CUTTER FLAG, CA. 1870 (ABOVE)

On this flag, a cotton muslin eagle and thirteen stars are configured onto the canton that is machine-sewn to the vertical stripes. At the fly end, some heavy wind-shear damage to the final white stripe can be seen. The flag has been folded to be photographed.

A UNITED STATES REVENUE CUTTER FLAG, CA. 1870–90 (RIGHT)

Here, an indigo-blue cotton eagle is sewn onto a white canton. On the bird's breast is a shield bearing seven red cotton stripes. There are thirteen indigo-blue machine-sewn stars arranged in an arch above the eagle. The body of the flag consists of sixteen alternating vertical red and white machine-sewn wool bunting stripes.

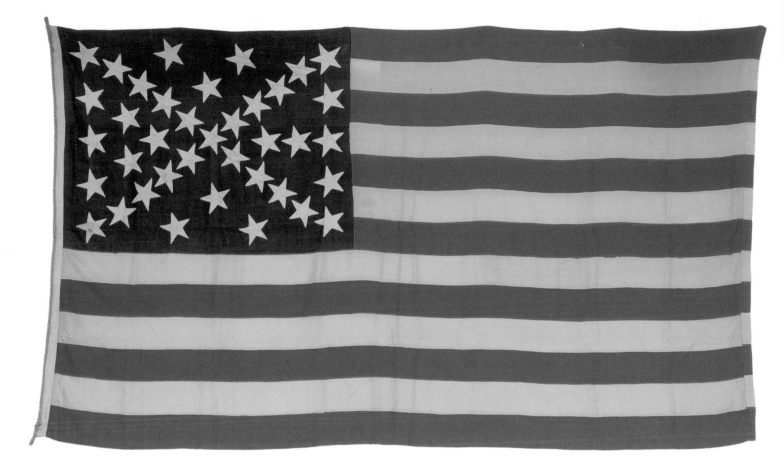

A "GENTLEMAN'S BOW-TIE" FLAG TO HONOR COLORADO, CA. 1876

The stars on this thirty-eight-star flag, which commemorates Colorado's admission to the Union on August 1, 1876, are set in a unique "Gentleman's Bow-Tie" design. A former owner wrote that ". . . the designer's attachment to the South as part of the reconstructed Union [is suggested by] the canton's bold saltire [which resembles] the Cross of St. Andrew," as seen on the canton of the Third Confederate National flag (see p. 54). The stars are cotton muslin, the canton and stripes, wool bunting. The entire flag is machine-sewn.

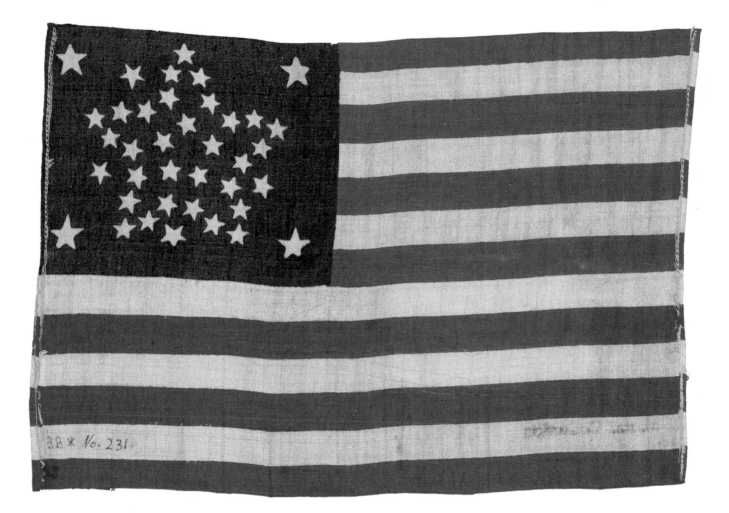

A "GREAT STAR" PARADE FLAG TO HONOR COLORADO, CA. 1876

This thirty-eight-star printed silk parade flag commemorates Colorado's admission to the Union in 1876. The stars are configured in a "Great Star" or "Great Luminary" pattern with stars placed between four of the five points; the whole design is flanked by larger corner stars.

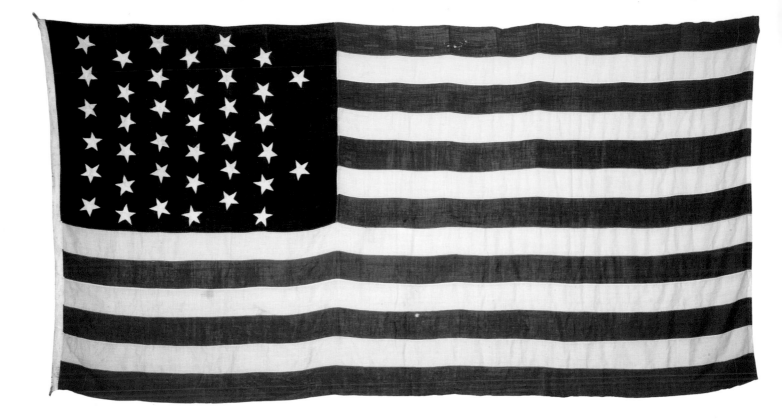

A FLAG TO HONOR COLORADO, CA. 1876

Colorado statehood flags seem to be more eccentric than most; of the nineteenth-century flags made to commemorate that state's admission to the Union, more of these thirty-eight-star flags exhibit unusual star configurations than do the flags of any other state. On this example the stars are set in vertically off-set rows that seem to ripple across the canton. The flag has a sailcloth canvas sleeve containing a period hemp rope, which indicates that it was probably made for nautical use. The stars are hand-sewn cotton muslin; the canton and stripes are machine-sewn wool bunting.

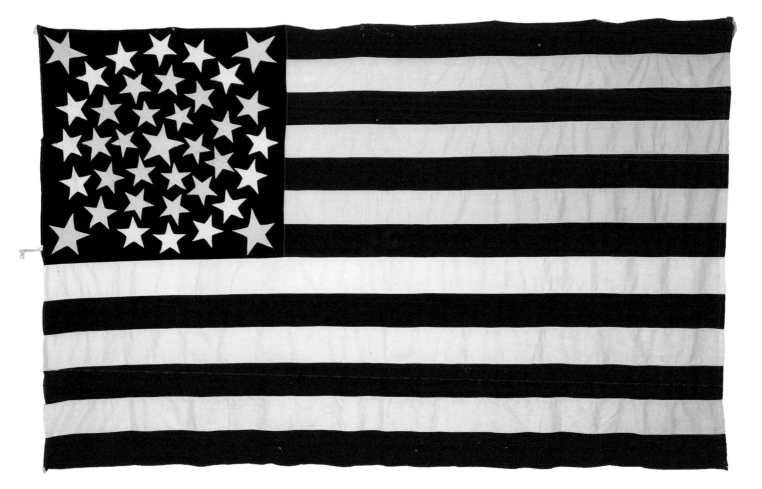

A TRIPLE-WREATH FLAG TO HONOR COLORADO STATEHOOD, CA. 1876

An interesting feature of this flag is that it is one-sided: There are no stars sewn on the reverse of the canton. Thus, it was intended to be displayed indoors rather than flown in the wind. The thirty-eight-star banner commemo- rates Colorado's 1876 admission to the Union. The stars are set in a triple-medallion pattern made up of stars of four different sizes, with a large central star to represent the new state. The entire flag is machine-sewn cotton.

On this flag the hand-sewn stars are set in a wreath or medallion surrounding a large central star and flanked by corner stars. The cotton stripes are both machine- and hand-sewn. This flag was probably made for the Centennial celebration of our nation's independence in 1876.

**A "PHILADELPHIA PATTERN" COLORADO
STATEHOOD FLAG, 1876 (RIGHT)**

This thirty-eight-star Colorado statehood flag features a double-wreath or double-medallion configuration of stars known as the Philadelphia pattern. Most commonly used during the Civil War, the double wreath is oval in form, with a large central star representing the new state, and the entire group is flanked by corner stars. During the third quarter of the nineteenth century, the use of this pattern began to decline. In this example, the stars are machine-sewn cotton muslin, the canton and stripes are wool bunting, and the sleeve is cotton.

A PARADE FLAG MADE FOR THE CENTENNIAL OF AMERICAN INDEPENDENCE, 1876

This parade flag was kept as a souvenir of the 1876 Centennial celebrations in Philadelphia. Its five-pointed stars are each accented by an additional ray extending between each point of the star, which gives a twinkling effect to the dates *1776* and *1876*. The printed canton was machine-sewn to the printed stripes; the entire flag is made of a cotton-linen blend.

A JAMES G. BLAINE CAMPAIGN FLAG FOR THE PRESIDENTIAL ELECTION OF 1884

James G. Blaine was the unsuccessful Republican presidential candidate in the election of 1884. This printed cotton parade flag features a portrait of Blaine in a central cartouche superimposed and partially obscuring the stripes and some of the stars in the canton. Campaign flags like this one are rare.

HANCOCK & ENGLISH.

Benjamin Harrison was the successful Republican presidential candidate in the election of 1888. The canton of this unusual campaign flag is a printed cotton bandanna bearing the names of Harrison and his vice-presidential co-runner, Levi Parsons Morton. After printing, the bandanna was attached to the thirteen stripes of a machine-sewn flag. This is a unique example of its type.

The legend *Hancock & English* painted across the fly end of this flag refers to Winfield S. Hancock, the unsuccessful Democratic presidential candidate in the election of 1880. The design of the flag is unusual: The pieced canton is white, and the thirteen stars scattered across it are of calico. The white stripes are much wider than the red ones, which, with the calico stars, gives this banner a distinctly "folk art" quality. The canton and white stripes are of cotton; the red stripes are wool bunting.

1876

A UNIQUE DOUBLE-SIDED FLAG TO HONOR ADMISSION
OF THE DAKOTA TERRITORY TO THE UNION

On November 2, 1889, the Dakota Territory was admitted to the Union as two separate states—the thirty-ninth and fortieth—North Dakota and South Dakota. This unique double-sided flag commemorates that event with thirty-nine stars on one side of the canton and forty on the other. The hand-sewn four-sided cotton muslin stars are set in a swirling irregular dou-ble-medallion pattern surrounding a large central star on a tiny cotton canton. The stripes are elongated machine-sewn cotton. Two unusual features are that the uppermost of the eleven stripes is white, and the bottom stripe is embroidered with the date 1876. It should be noted that there are only three surviving nineteenth-century flags that bear four-pointed stars.

A FLAG TO HONOR MONTANA STATEHOOD

This forty-one-star national flag commemorates
Montana's admission to the Union on November 8,
1889. The hand-sewn cotton muslin stars are configured in a "global scatter" pattern on a cotton canton.
Some flag collectors believe that when the canton sits
on a red "war" or "blood" stripe, it signifies that the
nation was at war and its soldiers were shedding their
blood when the flag was made. If that is so, the blood-
shed referred to here would be in the battles of the
closing years of the Indian Wars. During the nineteenth century, the various territories competed to
see which would attain statehood first. Since Washington was granted admission to the Union on
November 11, 1889, this forty-one-star flag honoring
Montana would have been valid for only three days.

A RARE TRIPLE-MEDALLION FLAG TO COMMEMORATE WYOMING'S ADMISSION TO THE UNION

Washington was to have become the official forty-second
state by order of Congress on July 4, 1890. But Idaho
stole some of Washington's thunder by gaining admission on July 3 of that year so that it became the official
forty-third state on what was to have been Washington's
day. But then Wyoming, in turn, seized center stage by
being admitted to the Union as the forty-fourth state
only seven days later, on July 10. Unusual for the late
nineteenth century, this flag features stars arranged not
just in a medallion, but in the even more rare triple-
medallion pattern. The machine-sewn cotton muslin
stars are set against a wool bunting canton. The stripes
are machine-sewn wool bunting. In this photograph, the
flag is shown folded in on itself several times.

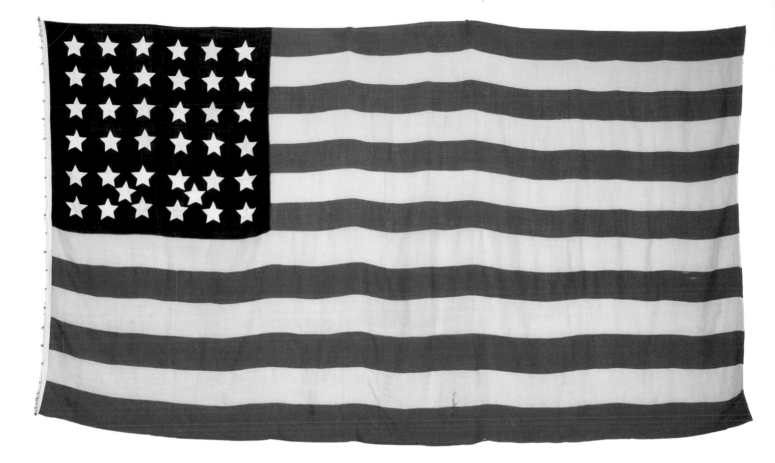

A FLAG TO HONOR COLORADO, 1876-1889

The "plump starfish" stars on the canton of this thirty-eight-star flag, which commemorates Colorado's admission to the Union in 1876, are configured in a geometric block of six rows of six each, with the two "extra" stars set between the fifth and sixth rows. The stars are hand-sewn cotton muslin on a pieced wool bunting canton; the stripes are machine-sewn wool bunting.

A FLAG TO HONOR WYOMING

This forty-four-star American national flag commemorates Wyoming's admission into the Union on July
10, 1890. The hand-sewn cotton muslin stars are configured in a double-medallion pattern with a large
central star representing Wyoming on a cotton canton.
Some flag collectors believe that the canton resting on
a red "war" or "blood" stripe indicates that our country's soldiers were shedding their blood in the closing
years of the Indian Wars. This flag was made for a ship
captain's family from Maine, possibly indicating the
family's prior military service during the Civil War,
when this configuration was more common.

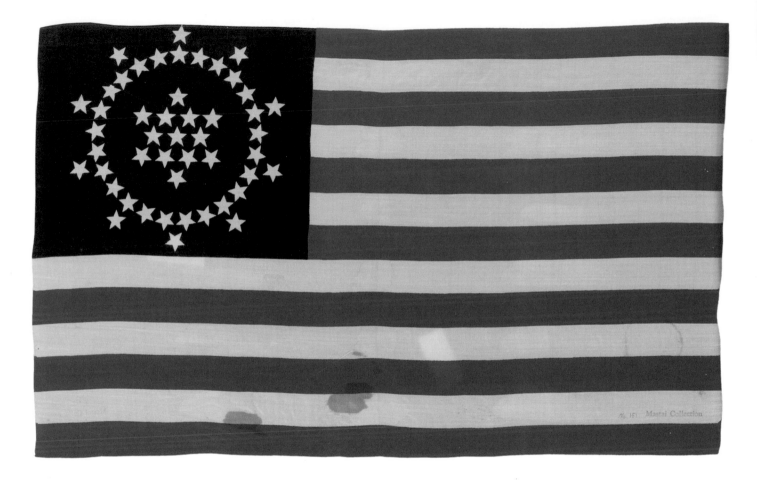

A 48-STAR WHIPPLE PARADE FLAG, CA. 1912

This unusual version of the "Great Star" flag was created in 1912 as an entry to a design contest by Wayne Whipple, an author of popular books on American history. In the center of the canton is a "Great Star" made up of thirteen stars representing the thirteen original states. The twenty-five stars arranged in a ring around it represent the states admitted to the Union up to the time of the First Centennial celebration in 1876. Finally, an outer ring—which leaves space for later additions—represents the states admitted after the Centennial. This example, a parade flag, was printed on silk.

A NINETY-STAR PATRIOTIC OR POLITICAL BANNER, CA. 1896—1907

The printed canton of this flag consists of an uncut pair of forty-five-star flag cantons that have been machine-sewn to six alternating red, white, and blue cotton stripes. The words *U.S. Jack* are printed in the mid-section of the canton. The words refer to a naval jack—essentially a canton without stripes—a small flag used on American ships. This late nineteenth-century banner may have been used at a naval celebration during the Spanish-American War of 1898—99. It is one of only two American flags known that feature stripes in red, white, and blue.

A "BIBLE" FLAG FROM WORLD WAR I

Beginning with the Civil War, a soldier would carry, tucked in his Bible or wallet, a small remembrance flag made by or given to him by his mother, wife, or sweetheart. This custom continued through World War I. This small (11-x-14-inch) forty-five-star flag was probably carried by a member of the American Expeditionary Forces while serving in France during World War I. It is inscribed: *First Train with American Prisoners of War Passed Through Lausanne on Friday Nov. 29th 1918.*

On June 24, 1912, the laissez-faire tradition of American flag design came to an end when President William Howard Taft issued an executive order establishing the proportions of the national flag's field and canton, and the arrangement and orientation of the stars. This order applied to the forty-eight-star flag—the most recent additions being New Mexico (January 6,1912) and Arizona (February 14, 1912) —that became official on July 4 of that year. The forty-eight-star flag remained the single official configuration for the American national flag for forty-seven years, carried by American soldiers in both world wars and the Korean War. It was finally superseded by today's fifty-star flag, which was described in an executive order of President Dwight D. Eisenhower dated August 21, 1959, the day Hawaii became a state. The new flag, which acknowledged Alaska's statehood (June 30, 1958) as well, became official on July 4, 1960.

This forty-eight-star cotton flag, a typical example of everyday mass production, was presented to one Israel Smith when he became a U.S. citizen at the age of twenty-one, in about 1927. He never parted with it and it was among his possessions when he died.

★

EDITOR: Elaine M. Stainton
DESIGNER: Allison J. Henry
PRODUCION MANAGER: Stanley Redfern

Photographs courtesy of Sotheby's, Inc.
Flag on page 79: Courtesy, Beck Archives of Rocky Mountain Jewish History,
Penrose Library and CJS, University of Denver

Library of Congress Cataloging-in-Publication Data

Druckman, Nancy.
American flags : designs for a young nation / Nancy Druckman;
with commentaries by Jeffrey Kenneth Kohn.
p. cm.
ISBN 0-8109-4506-1
1. Flags—United States—History.
I. Kohn, Jeffrey Kenneth.
II.Title.

CR113 .D78 2003
929.9'2—dc21
2002152403

Printed and bound in China

10 9 8 7 6 5 4 3 2 1

Harry N. Abrams, Inc.
100 Fifth Avenue
New York, N.Y. 10011
www.abramsbooks.com

Abrams is a subsidiary of
LA MARTINIÈRE
GROUPE

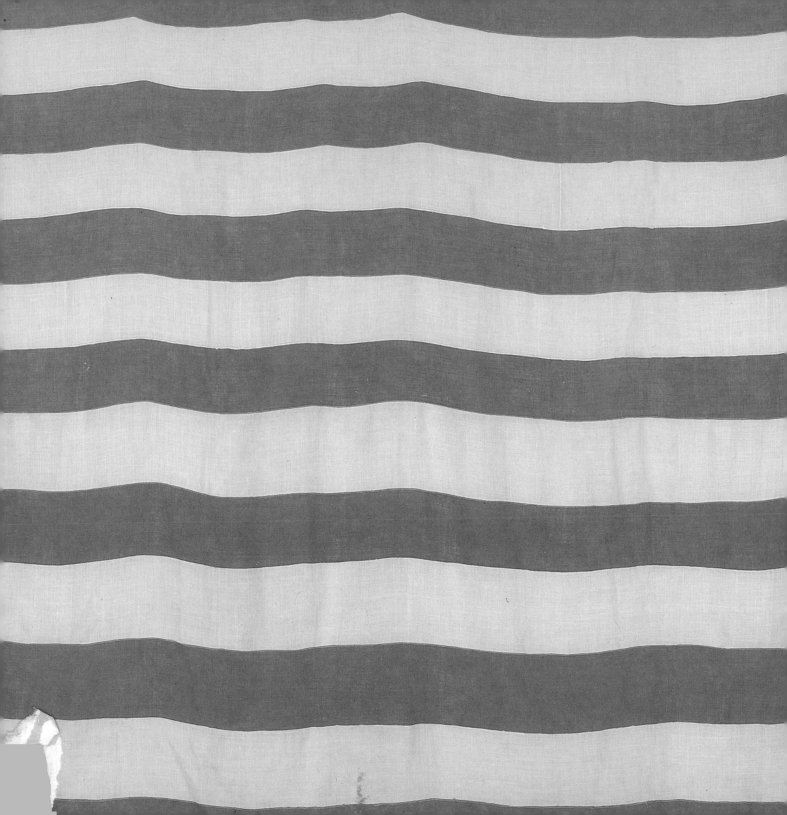